W9-CCB-433

NO LONGER THE PROPERTY OF
BALDWIN PUBLIC LIBRARY

14.95

Fiber

by Jane Inglis

Carolrhoda Books, Inc./Minneapolis

BALDWIN PUBLIC LIBRARY

Words that appear in **bold** are explained in the glossary on page 30.

Illustrations by John Yates
Cartoons by Maureen Jackson

Photographs courtesy of: Aspect, p. 9; Cash, pp. 11 (top), 22, 25; Cephas, p. 20; Chapel Studio, *Cover*, pp. 5, 6, 8, 11 (bottom), 12, 15, 21; Bruce Coleman, pp. 7, 24; Jeff Greenberg, p. 4; Tony Stone, p. 19; Zefa, pp. 18, 29.

This book is available in two editions:
Library binding by Carolrhoda Books, Inc.
Soft cover by First Avenue Editions
241 First Avenue North
Minneapolis, Minnesota 55401

First published in the U.S. in 1993 by Carolrhoda Books, Inc.
All U.S. rights reserved. No part of this book may be reproduced or transmitted in any form or by any means, electronic or mechanical, including photocopying and recording, or by any information storage or retrieval system, without the prior written permission of Carolrhoda Books, Inc., except for the inclusion of brief quotations in an acknowledged review.

Copyright © 1992 Wayland (Publishers) Ltd., Hove, East Sussex. First published 1992 by Wayland (Publishers) Ltd.

Library of Congress Cataloging-in-Publication Data

Inglis, Jane.
    Fiber / by Jane Inglis.
        p.   cm.
    Includes bibliographic references and index.
    Summary: Identifies what dietary fiber is and discusses its importance and its sources. Includes recipes and related activities.
    ISBN 0-87614-793-7 (lib. bdg.)
    ISBN 0-87614-608-6 (pbk.)
    1. Fiber in human nutrition—Juvenile literature.
[1. Fiber in human nutrition.] I. Title.
TX553.F53I53   1993
613.2'8—dc20   92-34143
                                                                  CIP
                                                                  AC

Printed in Belgium by Casterman S.A.
Bound in the United States of America

1   2   3   4   5   6   98   97   96   95   94   93

Contents

371 236d

What Is Fiber?

A fiber is a thin thread. Fibers are found in plants. Each thread is made up of tiny things called **cells** that are invisible to our eyes. Every living thing is made from cells—even us.

The cells of the plants we eat are like packages wrapped in fiber. Inside a cell are the **nutrients** our bodies need to keep healthy.

The outside of a cell, or cell wall, is made up of fiber. This fiber helps plants stand up just as our skeletons hold our bodies up.

There are two kinds of fiber in plants—**crude fiber** and **dietary fiber.** Most crude fiber is taken from wood or cotton and made into cloth or paper. Dietary fiber is the kind that we

ABOVE
How healthy is the food you eat?

RIGHT
These foods are made with whole grains and are high in fiber.

4

eat. This fiber is an essential part of our **diet.**

Meat contains no fiber. Neither do dairy products or any other foods that come from animals. All the fiber that we eat comes from plants, although some plants have more fiber than others. **Cereals**—grains such as rice, wheat, and oats, and the products made from them—are very high in fiber. Nuts, fruits, vegetables, and **legumes** are also good sources of fiber.

ABOVE
*Peeling vege-
tables not only
removes a lot
of fiber, it also
removes many
of the valuable
vitamins and
minerals which
are stored just
beneath the skin.*

Most of the fiber we eat is found in the outsides, or skins of the fruits, grains, and vegetables we eat. Much of this fiber is lost when the outside layer is removed. This is what happens when fruits and vegetables are peeled, white flour is milled, sugar is taken from sugar beet or cane, and oil is pressed from nuts and seeds. These products come from the inside part of the plant, which has the most nutrients. But the skins and husks—the valuable fiber—are often thrown away or used to feed farm animals.

Food which has been treated in this way is called **processed food.** Factories package or can this food to be sold in stores. It is not as good for us as it was before it was processed. When the outer parts of plants are

fruits have more fiber than a single strawberry.

Different kinds of fiber are found in different plants, but they are all important. We need to eat a variety of foods for a good balance of fiber in the foods we eat. This book explains why this is so, why so many of us do not eat enough fiber, and how we can increase the amount of fiber in our diets.

BELOW
Raspberries are a good source of fiber and are delicious.

thrown away, fiber, vitamins, and minerals are wasted.

Raspberries and blackberries are high in fiber. This is not surprising, since the outsides of fruits contain more fiber than the insides. Look closely at a raspberry or blackberry. Each berry is made up of lots of tiny pieces joined together. Each piece has its own skin all around it, so these

Science Corner

We cannot always tell by looking at food, or even by eating it, whether it contains a lot of fiber. But natural, chewy foods that take a while to eat are usually high in fiber. Take a close look at some dried figs, prunes, or apricots. All of these contain a lot of fiber. Wash your hands, then cut a piece of fruit open and look at it through a magnifying glass—or better yet, a microscope. Feel the texture with your fingers. You should be able to see and feel lots of tiny threads.

After cutting up the dried fruit, eat it! Figs, prunes, and apricots are sweet and tasty. It takes a while to chew them. Their texture, and the time it takes to eat them, are clues to the high amount of fiber they contain.

The History of Fiber

Before the days of farming, people lived off the land, gathering wild plants to eat and hunting animals. A lot of their food came from plants because plants were easier to catch than animals! This food was full of fiber. People ate wild grass seeds, nuts, berries, and fruits.

These people used the wild grass seeds to make bread. They pounded the seeds with rocks, added water, and cooked their flat bread on a stone in the sun. They discovered they could plant seeds to grow new grains for bread, and they no longer had to gather wild seeds.

Early millstones, or stones used to **mill,** or grind grain into flour, have been found where these early people lived. A hole through the middle of one

ABOVE
This tree is loaded with apples. When we buy our food from grocery stores, it is easy to forget where it actually comes from.

Investigation

Would you survive in the wilderness if you had to live without processed food? Make a list of of the fruits and nuts you know are safe to eat. Many berries and mushrooms are poisonous, so you would have to be careful. Would you have enough to eat?

stone allowed the grain to fall onto a flat stone underneath. The top stone was then turned by hand, and the grain was crushed between the two stones. Flour made this way had as much fiber in it as the grain itself because nothing was removed from the grain.

The color of the bread made with these whole flours was brown, and the bread was heavy and flat. But the Egyptians discovered that they could add **yeast** to dough before it was cooked to make the bread rise. This bread was much lighter and softer—and easier to chew.

Through the ages, people found many different ways to make milling flour easier.

LEFT
Windmills use power from the wind to turn the millstones, which grind grain into flour.

BELOW
Outside this water mill, a huge wheel is turned by falling water and moves these gears inside.

Animals and the power of wind and water were all used to turn the millstones.

People have been grinding flour and eating bread for centuries. Every culture eats some form of bread, and it is one of the most widely eaten foods in the world even nowadays. Bread can be very different from country to country. Pita, tortillas, bagels, baguettes, biscuits, chapatis, corn bread, and muffins are just a few of the many types of bread you may like to eat.

White bread

In ancient Egypt and Rome, people discovered a way to make white bread, which was softer and lighter. Only rich people ate this bread—it was expensive to make. Sometimes white powders, such as chalk, were added to whiten the flour. But usually the whole grain flour was sifted through cloth to take out the germ and husk, or outsides, of the grain. These skins are what makes bread brown—and rich in fiber. This bread was not as pale as the white bread we eat today, because not all the fiber could be removed by sifting.

Most people could not afford to buy this kind of bread and continued to eat dark, whole grain bread. We now know this dark bread was

healthier than white bread because it contained a lot of fiber and nutrients.

Processed foods

Some people continued to eat white bread over the years, but it was not until the 1800s that a method was invented to make large amounts of white flour. New mills used large rollers to grind grain into flour and take wheat germ and husk out of the flour. This flour made bread that was very white and could be produced in large quantities, so more people could afford it.

Unfortunately, this meant that the diet of poor people became less healthy. They had always eaten a lot of bread because it was cheap, but now it was lower in nutrients and fiber. They liked this soft, white bread, but they did not know that it was not as good for them as brown bread.

White flour is only one example of a processed food. Many other crops now go straight from the fields to factories. Here they are separated by machines into the parts used for human food and the leftovers.

White sugar is made from sugar beet or cane. Much of the bulky material left over from making the sugar is fed to animals. Rice, the main food of millions of people in the Far East, is usually polished to remove the outer layer. Whenever food is processed, fiber is one of the most important things that is lost.

13

Science Corner

This is a diagram of the inside of a grain of wheat. Can you find the fiber? If you were to cut open a grain of wheat and look at it with a magnifying glass, this is what you would see.

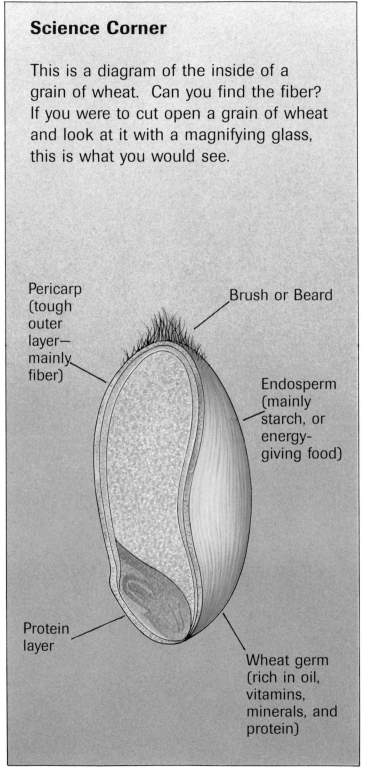

Pericarp (tough outer layer— mainly fiber)

Brush or Beard

Endosperm (mainly starch, or energy- giving food)

Protein layer

Wheat germ (rich in oil, vitamins, minerals, and protein)

When you see how much goodness is wasted when food is processed, you may wonder why we keep processing food. There are several reasons. Freshly grown food straight from the garden or field is best for us. But most people live in towns or cities far from the fields where food is grown. Food has to last a long time to get from the field to our table, and fresh food rots quickly. Food is shipped all over the world, and once it is processed, it lasts longer. For example, whole wheat flour contains oil from the germ of the wheat, but this oil goes bad quickly. White flour, which does not have this oil, lasts much longer.

People in our modern world are used to eating food that does not take long to prepare. Processed food often takes less time to cook than whole grains and vegetables. Also, food manufacturers make more money from processed, ready-made meals than from selling whole foods. For example, look at the weight of a package of potato chips. How much would the same

LEFT
Nuts and raisins make a delicious snack and are a healthy alternative to candy and chips.

weight of potatoes cost if you bought them at a grocery store? Whole potatoes cost very little compared to what you paid for the potato chips. And the chips have had their skins—and all their fiber—removed, and salt, fat, and chemical flavorings added, so they are not as healthy as the whole potatoes.

Advertising helps persuade people to buy processed foods. Once we are used to a certain kind of food, it takes time and effort to change our eating habits.

Recipe

Use this recipe to make your own whole wheat bread. It is easy to make, delicious to eat, and, of course, full of fiber. Make sure an adult is present when you are cooking.

Ingredients

2½ cups whole wheat flour
1 teaspoon baking soda
½ teaspoon salt
1 teaspoon baking powder
½ teaspoon cinnamon

½ cup honey
¼ cup oil
1½ cups buttermilk
½ cup chopped walnuts
½ tablespoon grated orange peel

Equipment: large mixing bowl, measuring cups and spoons, wooden spoon, one 9 x 5 inch loaf pan or two 7 x 3 inch loaf pans, greased with butter or margarine

1. Mix ingredients together in the order they are listed. Beat well.
2. Spoon dough into greased pan or pans.
3. Turn oven on to 375°F.
4. Let dough stand for 20 minutes.
5. Bake larger loaf for 45 to 60 minutes or smaller loaves for 30 minutes. Bread should be brown on top. To check if the bread is done throughout, poke a knife in the middle of the loaf down to the bottom. If the knife comes out clean, the bread is done; if it comes out with dough on it, it needs to bake a bit longer.
6. Remove bread from pan or pans to cool.

Why Is Fiber Good for You?

This diagram shows the human **digestive system.** All the food we eat is broken down as it goes through this long, twisty passage, and the nutrients our bodies need are taken out along the way. The food that is not **digested** passes through our bodies as waste. Most of this undigested food is fiber. Fiber does the very important job of helping to keep the digestive system working.

Digestion starts in the mouth. There, saliva mixes with the food to start breaking it down as it is chewed into pieces small enough to be swallowed. Then it goes down the throat into the stomach. **Acids** start breaking the food down further, churning it into a smooth paste.

Muscles in the walls of the stomach squeeze the paste down into the small intestine. Here the food is broken down by more juices into tiny particles small enough to pass through the walls of the intestine.

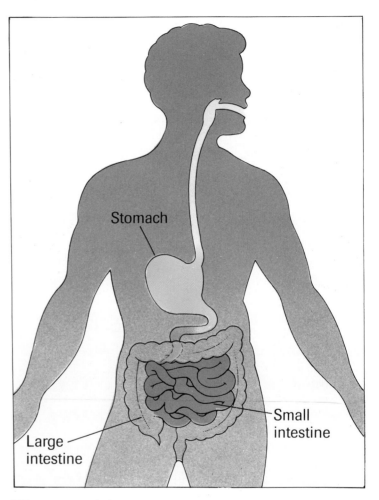

Stomach

Large intestine

Small intestine

These particles are carried by the blood to all parts of the body to be used to help our bodies work and grow.

The last part of the tube is the large intestine. By the time food arrives here, most of what the body can use has been digested.

ABOVE
*Eating beans
and peas is a
great way to
increase the fiber
content of your
diet. Beans
don't have to
be boring—the
variety of shapes,
colors, and tastes
is amazing!*

The rest is waste, and the sooner the body gets rid of it, the better. It is no longer useful and, like everything that was once alive, it will rot. This can produce poisons which may harm the body.

At the end of the digestive system is a storage area for waste called the rectum. When enough waste has piled up in the rectum, we pass the waste, or stool, through an opening called the anus.

People who eat a lot of fiber will be able to digest their food and get rid of waste quickly and easily. People who have high-fiber diets are much less likely to become **constipated,** or unable to pass waste, than people who eat lots of processed foods.

Scientists measure how long it takes waste material to leave the body after it has been eaten. This is called **transit time.** The transit time is longer for processed foods than for foods that contain a lot of fiber. A short transit time is best because there is less chance for poisons from the waste to harm the body.

Transit time is different for different people, depending on what they eat and how they live. Transit time can vary from eight hours to two weeks. People living in rural villages in poor countries have a transit time of about one and one-half days. Healthy people living in wealthy countries have an average transit time of about three days. Some elderly people may have a transit time of two weeks.

LEFT *Try to do some exercise each day. This will help your digestive system work better.*

Why is there such a difference in the time it takes people to digest food? People who live in rural villages and grow their own food or buy it from the grower most often have high-fiber diets. These people who eat mainly whole vegetables and cereals and very few processed foods will have a shorter transit time.

People in wealthy countries eat a lot of meat and other animal products that contain no fiber at all. The cereals they eat are often processed and have lost much of their fiber. Most of their food is grown a long way from where they live, so it must be processed in order to stay fresh.

Exercise also makes a difference in transit time. Elderly people often exercise less than young people. This is bad for their digestion as well as for their general health. Also, muscles tend to get weaker with old age—even the digestive muscles. This will often slow the digestive process for elderly people.

BELOW
This meal of rice and chopped vegetables contains many of the ingredients necessary for a healthy diet.

ABOVE
*Dried fruits,
such as these
currants, raisins,
and apricots are
especially high in
fiber and make
a good snack.*

Digestive problems

A person who has eaten only low-fiber foods for many years may have problems with constipation. Digestive problems over many years can cause serious illnesses, such as **colon** cancer. This deadly disease is almost unknown among people from villages in poorer countries with high-fiber diets. It is much more common in rich countries where processed foods are eaten regularly.

A high-fiber diet is also less likely to cause our teeth to decay because these foods generally have less sugar. And it is more difficult to eat too much fiber since it is bulky and fills the stomach, making us feel full longer. All of us could probably eat more fiber, and adding more to our diets is easier than you might think.

How to Increase the Fiber in Your Diet

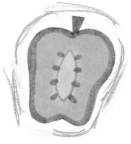

of white rice, choose brown rice. Brown rice takes longer to cook, but it's worth the wait. Most supermarkets sell whole wheat pasta as well as the usual white kinds. Try couscous or bulgur instead of pasta or rice for variety. Pastries, cookies, and cakes can be made with whole wheat flour—and still taste delicious.

BELOW
These mouth-watering vege-table burgers have been made using high-fiber ingredients.

When scientists first realized how important fiber was, people began to add **bran,** the outer covering of cereal grains, to food as a quick way to eat more fiber. Bran is an excellent source of fiber, but we need fiber from a variety of different sources. And it is much better to eat fiber in its natural forms than to add bran to processed foods.

This means eating more whole foods and fewer processed foods. Instead of white bread, try eating whole wheat, rye, or pumpernickel bread. Instead

Recipe

Try this tasty recipe for brown rice pilaf. It is quick to make and full of fiber. Make sure an adult is present when you are cooking.

Ingredients

4-5 green onions
1 small onion
1 red pepper
1 green pepper
½ cup mushrooms

1 carrot
2 teaspoons vegetable oil
salt and pepper
¾ cup brown rice
2 cups water

1. Chop the vegetables into small pieces.
2. In a large frying pan, cook the chopped vegetables in the oil for about five minutes. Add salt and pepper.
3. Add the rice and stir for one minute. Pour on the water, turn the heat down, cover, and cook for forty minutes or until all the water is absorbed into the rice. Serve.

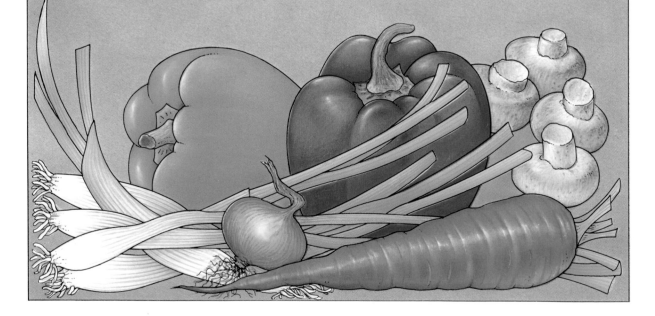

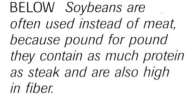

BELOW *Soybeans are often used instead of meat, because pound for pound they contain as much protein as steak and are also high in fiber.*

Where to find your fiber

For a high-fiber diet, we need to eat cereals, fruits, vegetables, and legumes. This may mean eating fewer animal products, such as meat and cheese. Animal products contain a lot of **protein,** the essential nutrient you need to grow. But you can also get protein from legumes, nuts, grains, and some vegetables—and you'll be eating lots of fiber, too.

Next time you are thirsty for a glass of fruit juice, try eating a piece of fresh fruit and drinking a glass of water instead. Eating the fruit rather than drinking the juice gives you more fiber, and fruit juices

BELEW *Be creative when you are deciding what to eat. This huge sandwich is full of fiber and other nutrients, and it tastes great.*

often contain added sugar. Try nuts or dried fruits for a healthy snack instead of chocolate or sweets.

Fresh vegetables and fruits vary in the amount of fiber they contain, so eating a lot of different kinds will give you the best mix of fiber. And fresh vegetables and fruits are full of a lot of other nutrients we need. As long as you wash fruits and vegetables well, or eat organically grown food that has not been sprayed with chemicals, it is best to eat the skins, too, because they are loaded with fiber.

This table lists some common foods and the amount of fiber there is in 100 grams of each. This is important to know when you are trying to increase the amount of fiber in your diet. Think about which foods you may want to eat more of.

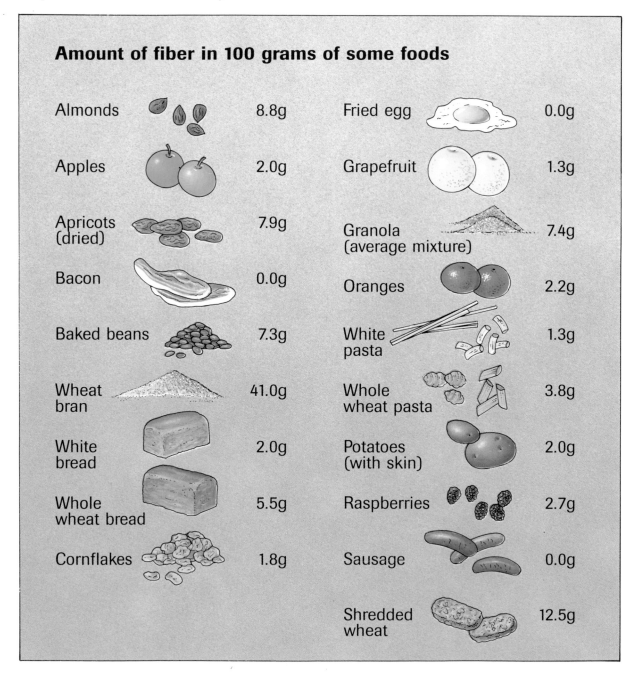

Amount of fiber in 100 grams of some foods

Almonds	8.8g	Fried egg	0.0g
Apples	2.0g	Grapefruit	1.3g
Apricots (dried)	7.9g	Granola (average mixture)	7.4g
Bacon	0.0g	Oranges	2.2g
Baked beans	7.3g	White pasta	1.3g
Wheat bran	41.0g	Whole wheat pasta	3.8g
White bread	2.0g	Potatoes (with skin)	2.0g
Whole wheat bread	5.5g	Raspberries	2.7g
Cornflakes	1.8g	Sausage	0.0g
		Shredded wheat	12.5g

Investigation

Look at these two breakfasts.
Which do you think is healthier?
Use the chart on page 26 to figure out how much fiber is in each one.
Turn to page 28 to find out if you have the right answer.

Breakfast One
Orange juice
Fried egg, bacon, and sausage
Two slices white toast with butter
and jelly

Breakfast Two
Half grapefruit
Shredded wheat cereal with yogurt
Two slices whole wheat toast with
raspberry jam

Science Corner

To find out how much fiber is in each of the breakfasts on page 27, we can figure out how much fiber is in each food, and then add it all together.

Breakfast One		**Breakfast Two**	
Orange juice	0.1g	Grapefruit	0.7g
Egg	0.0g	Shredded wheat	12.5g
Bacon	0.0g	Yogurt	0.0g
Sausage	0.0g	Whole wheat toast	5.5g
White toast	2.0g	Total	18.7g
Total	2.1g		

As you can see, Breakfast Two has much more fiber than Breakfast One. You can figure out how much fiber you ate for breakfast by using the chart on page 26 or by reading the side of your box of breakfast cereal. Most breakfast cereals, as well as other foods, list the amount of dietary fiber on the side of the package. You will also find other important nutrients listed, such as protein and vitamins.

   Most Americans eat about 15 grams of fiber a day. Experts believe people should eat 25-35 grams of fiber a day. We could all probably eat more fiber. Eating a breakfast like the second one would be a good start.

Bran contains more fiber than any other food on the list—fiber makes up nearly half of its weight. But it is very light, and 100 grams of bran is much more than most people would want to eat at once. To plan a high-fiber diet, you need to think about how much fiber is in normal helpings of the foods you want to eat. For example, potatoes do not contain large amounts of fiber, but we eat them so often and in such large quantities that they are a good source of fiber.

The more we know about the food we eat, the better we will become at choosing tasty, healthy meals. If we can make gradual changes toward eating more of the kind of food described in this book, we will be getting plenty of fiber, as well as all the other things we need to grow strong and healthy.

BELOW
Try making your own breakfast cereal. Think carefully about how to make it healthy and tasty.

Glossary

Acids Powerful liquid substances that help in digestion

Bran The outer skin of any cereal grain. Bran is rich in fiber.

Cells The tiny parts that all living things are made of

Cereals Edible grains, such as wheat, barley, and oats, and the foods made from them

Colon Part of the large intestine

Constipated Unable to pass waste

Crude fiber The threads found in plants, especially cotton and wood, that are made into paper or cloth

Diet All the food a person eats

Dietary fiber The threads found in the plants we eat. Dietary fiber is not digested and leaves our bodies as waste.

Digested When food is broken down into the parts our bodies need

Digestive system The parts of the body that break food down

Mill To grind grain into flour. Also, the building where flour is made

Legumes Peas and beans

Nutrients All the things in food that our bodies need to be healthy

Processed foods Foods that have been treated and changed from their natural state

Protein A nutrient found in foods such as meat, dairy products, nuts, and legumes that is an essential part of our diet

Transit time The amount of time it takes for food to leave the body as waste after it has been eaten

Vitamins Nutrients that help our bodies in many different ways

Yeast A fungus that is added to bread to help it rise

Books to Read

All about Bread by Geoffrey Patterson (Andre Deutsch, 1984)

Beans and Peas by Susanna Miller (Carolrhoda Books, 1989)

Bread by Dorothy Turner (Carolrhoda Books, 1989)

Good for Me!: All About Food in 32 Bites by Marilyn Burns (Little Brown and Company, 1978)

Vegetables by Susan Wake (Carolrhoda Books, 1989)

Metric Chart

To find measurements that are almost equal

WHEN YOU KNOW:	MULTIPLY BY:	TO FIND:
AREA		
acres	0.41	hectares
WEIGHT		
ounces (oz.)	28.0	grams (g)
pounds (lb.)	0.45	kilograms (kg)
LENGTH		
inches (in.)	2.5	centimeters (cm)
feet (ft.)	30.0	centimeters
VOLUME		
teaspoons (tsp.)	5.0	milliliters (ml)
tablespoons (Tbsp.)	15.0	milliliters
fluid ounces (oz.)	30.0	milliliters
cups (c.)	0.24	liters (l)
quarts (qt.)	0.95	liters
TEMPERATURE		
Fahrenheit (°F)	0.56 (after subtracting 32)	Celsius (°C)

Index

BALDWIN PUBLIC LIBRARY

3 1115 00371 2360

NO LONGER THE PROPERTY OF
BALDWIN PUBLIC LIBRARY

NO LONGER THE PROPERTY OF
BALDWIN PUBLIC LIBRARY

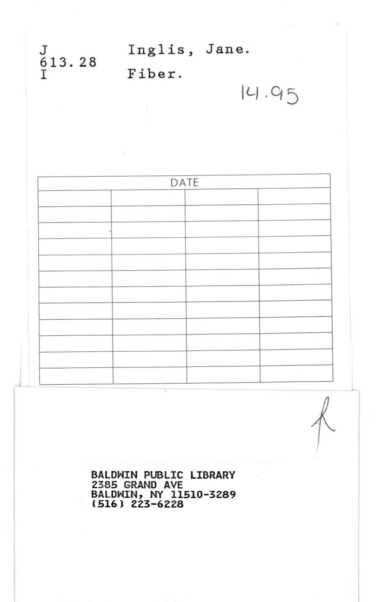

J   Inglis, Jane.
613.28
I   Fiber.

14.95

DATE			

BALDWIN PUBLIC LIBRARY
2385 GRAND AVE
BALDWIN, NY 11510-3289
(516) 223-6228

BAKER & TAYLOR BOOKS